The Hunger Wall

The Hunger Wall

(Hladová Zeď)

James Ragan

To Greg,
for your love of words
feeding the hunger
in your imagination —
Best Wishes,
James Ragan
Los Angeles
3-21-01

GROVE PRESS
New York

Grateful acknowledgment is extended to the following publications, in which these poems originally appeared: *Bohemian Verses, Anthology of Contemporary English Language Writings From Prague*: "Triad on the People's Road; *Bomb*: "Obsurity," "The Ossuary at Kutná Hora"; *Hampden-Sydney Poetry Review*: "Triad on the People's Road"; *New Letters*: "The Old Prague Jewish Cemetery"; *Trafika*: "The Hunger Wall"; *Troubadour*: "Crossing the Charles Bridge," "The Stone Steps to Hradčany," "The Siege."

Published simultaneously in Canada
Printed in the United States of America

FIRST PAPERBACK EDITION

Library of Congress Cataloging-in-Publication Data

Ragan, James, 1944–
The hunger wall (Hladová zed) / by James Ragan.—1st ed.
    p.   cm.
ISBN 0-8021-3478-5 (pbk.)
1. Bohemia (Czech Republic)—Poetry. 2. Slovakia—Poetry.
I. Title.
PS3568.A39H86   1995   811'.54—dc20   95-23561

Design by Laura Hammond Hough

Grove Press
841 Broadway
New York, NY 10003

10 9 8 7 6 5 4 3 2 1

For Tera, Mara and Jame,
whose hunger
feeds my imagination

I
Praha (Bohemia)

The Hunger Wall 5

Crossing the Charles Bridge 7

St. Jacob's Church of the Hanging Hand 9

The Old Prague Jewish Cemetery 11

The Ossuary at Kutná Hora 12

The Foreign Tourist Carrying the Antique Cross 14

Šárku 16

"Exclusive Photo with a Pretty Snake" 18

Obscurity 20

Triad on the People's Road 22

The Apostle Clock 24

The Stone Steps to Hradčany 26

Humenne (Slovakia)

The Separation 31

The Siege 33

The Period 36

The Handkerchief 37

Pietro the Fiddler 39

The Wedding 41

Bundling Clothes to the Old Country 45

Zivanska 47

The Walk 49

Reminiscing Joe 52

The Iconoclast 54

Huckster at Noontime 55

II
Yang-Na (Los Angeles)

Many Smokes 61

The Pacific 65

Olvera Street 66

Natural History 68

The Walls 69

A Glass of Claret 70

Hit and Run at the Pantages' 71

Shoplifting in a Korean Store 74

The Neighbor Who in Found Light 76

The Skinhead 78

The Docetist 80

Tajuta (Watts)

The Tower (Nuestro Pueblo) 85

Tar 87

A Drive-by on Saeegu 90

Dog in the Storm Drain at Florence and Normandie 91

Wrought Iron 93

Following the Juvenile Detention Bus 94

On the Day of His Death He Dreams 96

With Love the Infinite Is Passing By 97

Meliorism 99

Audienca 100

The Spearwort 103

Purgatorio 104

Notes 111

We are immersed in the now

that never stops blinking.

OCTAVIO PAZ

I

Praha

(*Bohemia*)

The Hunger Wall

You torment yourself, not knowing whether victory belongs
to the material or the immaterial aspect of the soul,
all the time feeling utterly alone,
separated by the dumb side of the wall . . .

VLADIMÍR HOLAN

The Hunger Wall

After walking to the bridge at Karlova,
we found the river where at dusk the swans
dipped their beaks into the falls for sanctuary.
The trees closed in for shade. We gazed
through willows to the opposite hill, a single
light from a room growing thick with sadness.
Solemn smoke now cooked the evening meal.

We were just about to treat our hunger well
when, out of sunlight, undeclared,
a shaded mass of stone began to stretch
its neck along the slope.
It would scan the water for a quarter hour
before the foliage rubbed its throat,
some internal hunger now assuaged

for only moments, then again, the impulse
thumbed like whalebone on a drum.
The poplars began to rustle. A hawk
spiraling, like an aspen deep in chatter,
betrayed its nest to block the sun.
The dam below rose up to boulder water
as if to show how easily wars are won.

They feed the hunger wall, the waitress points,
the fingers in her skirt rubbing coins

5//

her hand is shoring up to feed the past.
I don't want the poor to endure me, she says
King Charles said to those he paid, as he watched
their faces, building borders, hunger for a wall,
as she faced the smoldering Vltava, watching hunger well.

Crossing the Charles Bridge

Imagine a tunnel of stones,
dark, insinuating, a leap of walls.
Walk through it, without blinking.
Face the rood and river, the *Hrad*
gardens greening on your right,
to the left a waterfall
of swans that flurry into snow.
You will know the infinite
play of spires on the sky as light.
Night on every canvas will be painted red
and day the orange of rooftops.
Imagine every vine a map, every bridge
a branch to walk the Moldau larch
into the sun side of beauty.
Do not give in to blinking
or to thinking golems on the stair.
Imagine Kafka here at dusk, asleep
in the carrels of the Clementinum,
or sipping absinthe with Apollinaire,
or Seifert on the tram to Slavie,
every word a crick of tracks.
Imagine the future now dividing
wealth beyond the impulse into realm,
Libussa's olive trees at dawn,
a century of breath falling awake.

Imagine Havel with the sword of Bruncvik
stretching arms and legs
on the steps from Melantrich
to climb the Goldmaker's Alley,
the ghost of Rudolf on his back.

St. Jacob's Church of the Hanging Hand

He believed that touch
was a simple ride across a stream of velvet
at the skeining stall
or the sting of fire along brazed brass,
or when lightning cooled
in the wet sleep of a valley brook,
he had faith
in the promise of sensation,
the predilection of the body's mortal frame,
subdued, enraged as the hunger moved
to close the spaces
of what seemed to pass
and what, indeed, remained.

But nothing, no one
could predict the draft of terror
invading space so near the tattersall of jewels
the beggar's thumb had grasped.
What miracle of want
had fused his fingers to the Virgin's lace,
as if from an eternity of directions,
a hand or hands in cobra fashion
spiked his wrist,
and gaining force whipped
the venom into feral pitch?

No sooner had he dreamed at dawn
that in the cold posture of prayer,
a soldier's ax had freed his palm,
thought, the conscience vein,
was numbed to infinite suspension.

He remembered how before King Charles lay
in composition for the viewing mass,
he ordered all his fingers
sparred, to keep from being seized,
untombed into the darker death of neglect.
Above the reliquary
the beggar's bone, a deformed winch
propping up the vault of air,
points at the accused avenger. Opposite,
like a feeding plover wading light,
the Virgin, boasting pearls
as high as faith can rise,
tempts the heart of human nature
to face her mirror of greed.
No one breathes.
Should the statue move, all tombs will open.

The Old Prague Jewish Cemetery

The names appear through leaves like the driftings of crocus.
Occasionally, a stone hoists its prayer note
higher than the winch of knots along a linden root,
and a bole props the space between two rocks like a lean-to.
From a distance all rise like barks unhinged in a barren forest,
none higher or lesser in the corms of May.

Don't let the earth lie too heavy on the heart,
the rabbi prays in whispers mocking every stone.

He no longer believes in the martyrdom of silence.
What words he fails to say, each son or daughter,
alchemized by death, plants as monuments to sod.
At night they sleep in the darkness of their slopes.
Each time a mother picks cotyledon near the path at Terezín,
she breathes the *shem* of life into the mud and clay.

The Ossuary at Kutná Hora

The remains of 40,000 bodies of the wealthy decorate the Sedlec
monastery.

We have walked the pilgrimage well beyond
the wall's shock of cinders, to where the paths
are tributaries and skulls above the chapel
doors string out like party crepe.

And where we pay to see the bones of legend
breed in holy dust, a prayer booth
hawks a bunting of postcards. No one comes to pray.

The skulls that lost a nation, Hussite
boys, lie beneath their shells of mace;
the skulls in whose domes the bleached
odor of plague outlives the lime and soap

have soured down to stone. We are told a half
blind monk had gouged the sockets of their eyes
to build a pyramid of stairs to heaven.

We won't kneel beneath the altar's heap
to dig for silver relics. Or bow to hip bones
gripping the haloed gable. Our cameras pray
for light to keep from fading, for the canvas

of a boy appealing to the knees of grace
to keep from vanishing by permission
of the crown. What Bohemian prelate

gave to the earth its seal for engraving
such symmetry in death, the leisurely ascent
to form on ropes of femurs and fibulae?
Above the pulpit's stiff stair to faith,

a chandelier lights the exalted. There is no
room for the lowly in the frame of our lens.
Dying has a habit of running out of space.

The Foreign Tourist Carrying the Antique Cross

No doubt she is thinking as she packs
the bronzed arm snugly in the crate of her shoulders,
the body launched across the wedge of her spine,
how the wounds will sheen in the wash
of her pastel scarf,
                  that she will pray
for the will to repent the sins of the Reich,
and for what little faith molds deeply in her heart;
she will begin for the nation's sake
to kneel at the altar of her sink
and pail
                  and before the relic
polish the rusted nails and feet
like chrome she's bought on sale
from the antique dealer on Havelska Street
who kindly waves her, cross,
                  and who unkindly thinks
how, unlike the relic of the age she undertakes,
she will ride a limousine to Jalta's porch
and for the first few days admire, then forget
the sculpted veins of the neck, the sinews
of the thighs, the beauty
                  of its native metal

among those things she hopes to sell
or retire to the back hall of regret.
How cold the heart is; he thinks no further on it.
She thinks her mind will fail, that in the final
throes of breath, death will turn the profit.

Šárka

She is wearing the lathered marsh of wool
her sister Vlasta handed down
three days before she married. Hot
beneath an August moon, and wary
once of thighs disguised in pants, the Pilsen
girl now claims her tree at Wenceslas
with pride in breasts she's come with age to bare.

Her eyes are down the swans could seine,
her hands a saddle smooth as panty hose,
she leans against the music shop,
composed to writhe her body round
in some imaginary knot her mind has tied.
She has even willed the rain, enough
of boys, she wants emancipation

from all debris the conscience turns to lies.
And when a man approaching buys the horn
the window sells and plays it to the stars,
she arcs her spine as if to mint
his thumbs along her body's coinage.
All night the couple sways, negotiating
what if little of their minds they will exchange:

she with beaded breasts and pores,
he with borrowed notes to blow.

Neither knows how long till dawn the taxi
meter runs. No one hears the disco pound
in tempos far too clear for clarity.
When she talks of knives her sister carved
to hunt down boars, he wails

in longings old as Ctirad, loud as brass.
Her eyes, the carriers of age, already know
how roving men about the city
trumpet horns to lure the gypsy gyrals.
While native girls, unpracticed, growing old
build their mirrors above the beds at Devin
where every man, repenting blindness, prepares to pay.

"Exclusive Photo with a Pretty Snake"

It is August and along the tanks' slow crawl
swallows, high above the bald monk's hood,
leap the Charles Bridge to St. Francis
like phantoms out of animation. Angels
at his hip recite their fingertips to prayer.

A Prague teen panders souvenirs of Stalin.
Opposite his slate in chalk, *A Snake for Holding*,
a python girdles down the huckster's craw,
its fang excised to part the cusp and jaws.
It promises the neck a lustrous swim

of scales across the throaty swamp
of language. It hopes to numb the voice,
that by a glance or grisly yawn
eternal truths will bear no repetition.

Down the bridge a bus from Turin rivers out.
Shouts of fingers scale the saintly stones
for lines inscribed in Latin, and seeing
Greek in strict precision, they snub the basilisk.

Rock to rock they climb to flee the censor.
None will hold it. None demands a sound.
It wants attention, a brisk stroking or a pat.

No one bares his throat to the grip of its coiling
necklace. Swoons at lunch will follow eating

once it rolls adoring eyes and plays the pet.
St. Francis is not moved. He has tours to feed
as well as reputation. A snake has myths to keep,
and when it hisses, hardly a truth to bear repeating.

Obscurity

for Jan Zajíc (1950–1969), the second human torch to protest the 1968 Soviet invasion of Prague

There goes the night not knowing what
it is seeing. A boy has cut his lip shaving
and rinsed the basin free of blood
his hand had salved into the mind for no thought
in particular. At dawn he shot a heron.

He must have forgiven the debt his teacher
owed, perhaps, the promise of the moon
above his head forever, or a noun
his erratic tongue had failed to annunciate.

He might have counted as redemption
each lace of breath the girl had stroked
into his wailing hair at St. Vitus Lake.
He must have known. There ring the bells

he must have known were saved at Týn
for Palach, for the first to run; the pact
to torch imagination remembers only one,
no matter what the name, what the home.

He believed it is the found wisdom of an age
not to forgive the sins of a nation,

how the catacombs at Staré Město
age with molding chalk of poets' bones.

Here comes the imitator echoing stolen words.
Here runs the conspirator across the cat heads
of Karluv *most*, every rib of stone
a memory of loss, a birth into the every tongue,

saying there goes the wind not knowing what
it is hearing. There crawls a leaf, a moon,
and flames. There trips the clock's second hand,
which every moment tumbles deeper
into everywhere like a cough into a lung.

There goes a noun, unpronounced, into obscurity.

Triad on the People's Road

Ambushed, on the run, no thought to visit
death's attention or to cross the gauntlet

of Bartholomew's Black Hand, you lament
the penniless like a pocket's torn seam,

teeth gaping, cloth, full of voiceless drippings
from the rents of head wounds poems inflict.

In every age a poet dies in common
with a nation's brutal act; young Byron

roaming Greece for the eagle spirit's breath,
Pound for the countries dueling in his head.

One day you round a corner in the text
you call your verse, the next, you grow obsessed

with words, like thugs, not the least heroic,
who stalk you to the bend at *Národní*.

Loss is of no consequence to history
or police. Now the victims are the thieves

and the crime of passion belongs to all.
You might have bargained at an antique mall

for the sketch of a playwright, face between
two candles, watching a door, opening.

The entry is as clear as intention
in the drama the artist now begins.

The face does not exist nor the nation.
Thieves are at the door; art is illusion.

The Apostle Clock

You can sit near the oriel chapel
or on the Jan Hus cast,
the heretics rising tall
as wax in flames
of greening bronze,
to hear the Mozart *menuetto*
at the House of the Stone Bell
or near the House at the Minute,
where thousands stood as clock
stems in the Prague spring
to cheer Smetana's *Má Vlast*,
until, as usual, the hour
chimes across the Old Town Square,
and the skeleton of Týn
pulls the chain up
then round to shake the heads
of vanity and greed.
At the arm of Death
a Turk wags his chin.
An hourglass turns sideways down.
You can watch the tourists
draw in breath like Danes
to the stone of Tycho Brahe,
their hands above the eyes,
sycophants to changing time,

the astronomical trust
in earth's inspired motion
as the fleet of Prague's apostles
pose and spiral, impatient
imps, all wood and wise
to keep the sun and moon in union;
a cockerel flaps his wings
and caws for separation.

The Stone Steps to Hradčany

for Václav Havel

a

CHARLES BRIDGE

As I waltzed the *New World* to Hradčany
and did not feel in my feet
the pull-step of gravity
the low wall of wind denied me,
and did not hear among the spuds
of maple barks the asper tones
of a flutist's long wind whistle,
my eyes were drawn to eternity
in an inch of cobblestone. And counting
as if through each rasp of breath
I climbed the moated wall of Nepomuk
to reach communion with the sky's beginning.
I hurried through the strings
of marionettes, the jump-through stacks
of easel paints the gypsy cleaned,
and hurried past ensemble tombs
of Saints Xavier and Margarit,
the skein of clothes the fragile bag woman

drowsing on Neruda Street
spread affectionately
for little more than sun sleep
and little snores to do.

b

ST. VITUS

At the crest of St. Vitus beyond the Titan's Gate,
where spires, steep on the sky's slope,
formed their covenant with death,
I bowed deeply to the knees of gods imagined,
and by such mind genuflection,
breathed the swill of Parler's breath
up from the Seven Locks and down my throat.
I worshiped dust in shoes I half-stepped
to the jazz of grinders' stones.
At the crypt of Wenceslas,
where the vaulting soars, I prayed
to the rose mirror of all creation,
that faith in the planet's dream of life immortal,
began with wind in a spark of ocher.
I adored all stones on earth
and as they fell from heaven.

TEREZÍN

And with my hair soot red
as coals above my grandfather's bones,
buried near the poems of Desnos,
I hurried through the "Gate of Death,"
up the gallows' knoll,
the executioner's chiseled wall,
to see the Ohře rivering out
to wag the Elbe's long tail,
and hurried through the tunneled mounds
down again to hell,
past the fire's wind lash
of oven grates to holding cells
where brush wire and Jewish arms
in tubs of creosol
scrubbed all brains of the mind's eternal no.
In their bones the earth's push-step
the Aryan angel denied, moved me
to doubt in a changing world,
that all things, including stone, began
from one single Godly loss of breath.
On the slab at Terezín, in the "Lord's House,"
I climbed to bed, cold as heaven,
and played dead.

Humenne
(Slovakia)
The Separation

My Slavonic-Mongolian-Valachian soul loves conflicts with beings of different feelings; let it know itself, what it is, whether it can endure not in blindness and violence, but in tenderness.

DOMINIK TATARKA

The Separation

No one is seeding on the flats;
the path stopped growing,
the farmer whispers, beating the wheat
mold down with his hat.

Marriages are less, the walking
down to mere waves
from the rise of the hill.
We lost the road to the village,

we lost the will,
the words, the language
of a common dance. The mind
pulls only a single thread.

The road has nowhere to go
but through the narrowness
of needled grass
burnt to wisps of wilder.

Daily we stalk the corn,
and seeing loss, have found
the randomness of order
that stone breathes into land.

The field rolls over
to the ridge of its spine. It's easier
not to worry about creation,
to give up faith, than understand

indirection that drives a brother
lost in this hatred or that.
The farmer bows, weeding a road up
with his hands.

The Siege

for Andrew Jakuba (1880–1915)

You were six in the crawl rows
of cornstalks and aspen boles.
You remember your father leaning
from a horse, sartorial, a regiment
in pose. Everywhere you slept in winter
he would wake you. Any reason, any day.
Always the horse soldier, dying,
assuring, somewhere in the universe
north of the wheat, south of the rain,
the siege would end. So the mind forgets,
as the dream departs the stair
drawn down to bridge the waking,
how you wept beneath the willow
of his smile, to kiss the word's
last wave into the Crimean air.

The first dead letter came in May.
Six months, he wrote, the Ukraine ice
had spawned the final waters,
and strips of horse skin, the few remaining
carved to eat, swelled to stinking.
The Russians dare not cross the wall.
It is the human grace of longing

which trades the memory of a face
for the certainty of ground
that keeps an image home, alive,
in the soil of air drifting out
of boots, the epaulets, the busby warmth
of a soldier's hair; the elegance
of mourning as a daughter
no longer yours, you learn in time to regret.

Three years, in fact, before
his body flowered in the mind's
fertile earth. How the piglets squealed,
how the Angora hare and calves
kicked spring into eternal rounds,
the night the missionary aroused
the ghost of bones your father kept
alive in detention camps,
south of the Dnieper, north of your home.
A bower of chestnuts popped
in coals so red the leaves of his eyes
embalmed the fires, immortal.
So deep was your mother's wail
at the milking stool, the cows gave out.
You mourned the rain's tight pull
through lungs of his second breath,
so little in its borrowed time it crept
like the primal draw
of lace through a shoe's eye
before it broke.
                        You never spoke.

While written came his verse
no longer whistling to the elder blooms
in pastures of light. And whittled
fell the trunk of his branching bones
like oak that could no longer will him
to this earth and would not
when death was certain
rise again as hope.
                    And he remembered
to write a poem of *Bossi*, the gray
mare's hooves riddling out the jumping
rope you nettled in the barn;
and of *night*, how it wearied
of the moon caught in the underskirt
of darkness where you lay in wait
for the mare's newborn
scratching at the map of dirt.
How you'd leap to greet the door
light burst through, for any ghost
returning, sickly as a father,
with eyes and Christmas snows
as bleak as Pittsburgh coal,
bearing ornaments of crystal shells
for the years he passed in hell.
Here was the ground you were losing,
here was the siege of motion,
here was your hunger,
not the burnt silage in the meadows,
but the shoes of absence walking
in the absent air.

The Period

She recalled at twelve the laughter
of the village men in the field
where they forked the wheat, tossed
their sweat into the wells of hats,
slapped words out, to ring the sun's
creation dry of blame. In such laundry

of voices there came to her a bleeding
so unlike the heat and swell
she knew when cleansing
the grieved sliver of wood from beneath
a fingernail. In this forest of cries
she thought her own, she heard the low

whimper of flesh leave the womb in rivulets
that down the launder of her leg
seined to purify the seedlings.
She had thought this her body's rain,
recalling days each month she buried blood
in ground to raise her father. How to harvest

pain now that death she couldn't speak of
pulsed within her, relentless and maternal,
as if its seeding were a pasture growing,
laving through a field of orchids. How to lay
his memory down like the earth with persuasion,
saving shame alone as mother to her knowing.

The Handkerchief

On the secret map of sleep where she dreamed
she was in a cloister scooping off the wet weeds
of the garden she had raked with orange leaf through her hair,
the kerchief lay, embroidered silk

her mother soaked to cool her brow and throat. The fever
walked in circles through the eyes, fire nested in her feet.
Nowhere was the melody of dance she praised on waking.
Hardly had she heard the spring geese bray

to horses interloping down the hill at dusk,
when walking, a swift wrist riding the sweat from his brow,
he came, as promised, to her second dance, to muscle up
the brawling thugs who vowed to steal her breath.

The mother now had spoken. At fifteen years, don't toss
your willowed hair in golden dips along the swirling ground.
But giving all the chance she couldn't know
her mind was giving, she stole each offered hand

the boys declared, numbed as they were by fear
or simply heartbroken. The night was guilt and fevered.
Until the handkerchief was thrown, a band in silk
whose silver hurdled across the ballroom's sphere of stars.

The suitor now had spoken. As silently as thought
which skips the question to form an answer,
she walked to face him, one a mirror, the other forest.
She climbed as far and high into his mind as sleep,

then took his hand betrothed into the silk,
the sweat from each brow, a scent of oranges, commingling,
and dipping her willowed tress of gold across his eyes,
she scooped the wet weeds of the garden from his feet.

Pietro the Fiddler

He thumbs a blue roan from the village
lord, miles from the wedding. A bone-faced
gypsy, tongue screwed inside his lip,
fingers locked in catguts like tangled antlers,
he hangs his eyes from the fiddle's ribs,

wet as icicles. "Cigan," they call
across the combed sod floor of the parlor
where he dances the *doma*, strumming
beneath their vows the soft wood bark
of a birch, little more than a sapling.

Soon the dancers, trotting birds along the bow,
will knock their nostril beaks
against his brow, pocked and cleft
where thoughts have eaten out. "Cigan,"
they cheer at the Apollo's soft moon landing

as he strokes the taut strings bloody, notes
clotting in his mind, and acts the invited neighbor.
A virtuoso collating pitch on broken strings,
he plays the deaf-mute tapping thumbs to variations
on a theme. He will take his crowns and go

before the Armstrong leap for humanity, an apparition
wandering all the borders back into Romany,
where for a room he strums the *czardas*. And where
alone he walks the miles of space he calls his country,
an astronaut on the edge of solemn darkness.

The Wedding

I

Here was her bridal dance and there
her two sisters leaning,
cherry-cheeked, so triangular
you'd think the room was tilting,
perhaps a pine barrel rolling
underground, perhaps the *borovitsa*,
and the groom's brother waltzing
arm to arm and pausing only
for a round; all of them, trading
gain for loss, were the mannequins
she dressed to fit her gown,
the white so willing
to swash against the hickory pegs
and heartwood of feet crowding
in the days for one.
Here was their dance of lust,
Here, the last call's *redovy tanec*
to a virgin's kiss,
of lining up the week's small
salary for the downing of a shot.

Yes, he was held by tradition
out of sight, the groom,

far from the drunkard's tongue
now stabbing through the ice.
Yes, he would share her wheat
of hair this last time, each hot
lip fawning up her cheeks. Yes,
he would catch her eye just now;
it drips between the globes of roses.
Yes, yes, he would charge the locked
arms of the bride's maids and breaking
ties, prepare to lift
her face up and away from seeing
all the false force of the earth
spinning, the mother's feint
of feet as if to kneeling, the veil,
instinctive in its grace, tossed
up against the ceiling,
                    and the ice pick
that slices space just so
that vision caught in the spindle's rift
can rend its rage of oblivion
through his brother's eye, the rush
of arms to knuckle down
its parry, the drunkard leaping
past the spillage,
past the chambers of the pupil rivering
darkness onto wine.

II

            No, she only knelt
as if the lace were bleeding,
cradling now the brother's head,
her hair draping miles of language
he was feeding to the mind;
his memory, a chestnut
bough now breaking, his silence
only shaking through the shudder,
a flute returning wind to sound.
            No she didn't know
the groom, possessed,
had chased the demon *pan*
for days into the miles of spruce.
Yes, he might avenge
the assassin with an ax, within the inch
of breath the law allowed. No,
he chose to maim the raging eyes
as if the gendarme blessed
the rowel of briars,
            and all she could think of
was the eye turned black
on her white trousseau,
           and all he could think of
was to steal away beyond the walls
the guards had bribed
each night to open like a cask,

              and all she remembered
was her breath tossed like a river
rasping over rocks and the wet
weeds of her bed when he left at dawn,
              and all he remembered
was the year of nightly raptures,
and mourning in the cell he had grown
like stones around his head,
              and all that each remembered,
was the passion they had married
to the slow want of an embrace,
a bridal dance to death,
              two continents
adrift in a world racing
past the Archduke's carriage,
falling off its rims and spinning
slowly into ash.

Bundling Clothes to the Old Country

Had we known that in the eyes of the widow
the flannel wore its hunger less than the gabardine
or tamboured shirt or that Sunday rules no farmer,

and that her daughter's censoring finger
like a snake slighted by any outcropping of stitch
would wag and fang in dithering rejections,

we would have spared the monthly mailing of America,
sewn by mother's careful needle out of pillow halves
with boasting postage canceled on a field of white.

Each woolen shawl and sweater imploded like sponge.
Always the dollars stowed in socks or jersey hems
were tamped to regard the postman's grifting eye,

and threadbare legs of nylons, cut to strips,
were sculpted into rainbow threads of kitchen mats.
Here the letters lay with aspirin. Economies were slowing.

Handing down was handing up. And knowing who
was knowing how the herring tweed we posted
would be offered back as contraband or out of style,

45//

the exiled cousin wore it home as an apology
for the war he bartered, tugging in the streets.
He also wore the *visa* face on which the widow mirrored

our father's pose to pass him through the sensor's
border of illusion. Handing down was handing up,
and knowing who was knowing how to dress for freedom.

Zivanska

After the doors were shut and the windows sealed
to let the ember's soft foot lie, my father
slapped the crystal clear of wine and rising
tall as Janosik, full of heart, whispered down,

"Grass is burning. Stags are in the wood."

And out into the green night and salt arbors
of the brook we followed the king of bandits
upslope through the branched spires and thickets
into woods where only mold and roses thorned.

Under a moon as low as a mushroom scone,
we soured coals in sprigs and ginger grass
and hidden as with any intention the mind deceives to rob,
the sparks saw into the burning earth

what flint of fire could set the night to gasp.
A crackling sound began to grow into the roaring
hooves of deer and longer still to racing herds
as bacon fat dripped longingly into laps of bread,

and onions skewered and spat above the fire spears.
In my father's fist the long wind reed became a switch
that like the last finger on a hand hooked
potatoes by the eye. Wine took the aching down

into the throat and further in, the heart of something
shook that only nature recognized as sound.
The grass had burned to snapping darkness and to the last
sobbing tongue, my father pointed down to silence,

"The stags are gone. Boars have killed their young."

And no one moved. The king of bandits sheathed
his spearhead into ground. None had known
that hidden in the wet rock of the August clearing
a boar, alone and sorry for its breed, had moaned and wept.

The Walk

I

THE FATHER

She was his wife. Words were last to rub their sleeve
into the matter. First the eyes searched
the doors and lintels for the son he would not leave
to sing among the rabbit scuts and birch,

however stanched the blood they had in common;
he would not stand accused. For such a thing as trousers,
as to whom was gifted most or better, he summoned
all her family's crate of clothes, and while theirs

had been divided first, the better half
luxuriated in his sister's hand, according to a source
at the highest level of family greed. And someone laughed
to hear he'd rather pay them money than be cursed

by accusation. The whims of cloth are yours to own,
he said, while tabling up the coins to win his son.

2

THE HILL

Under the bruised blue cape of evening the moon
was what he gathered next and holding silence
by the wrist, pulled their weight along the highland's
tall cool greening, path into path leading nowhere but down
again to longing. Such is absence that it loses what is won.
No matter what the mailing, a pair of baled pants
or slippers, there's no telling how to balance
what needs paying to those who say they owe no one.

The boy could not catch up in years to know the pride
his father mailed in pillowed parcels, nor had bothered.
There was sky and clay to climb. At risk was reputation.
On the hill's wet slope something higher than the soul had died.
Down the willow's sleeve came the weeping; your father's
name, he said, is all you own, the rest is God's creation.

3

THE MOTHER

Staring long into the open stove to hear his name
repeat in silence, she folded memory like an apron
neatly on the grill. And palled to speak the rain's

odd language, she could not hear the nation's
tongue her mother loaned her for the road, nor the raven's
mocking wing above the kale and mallows.
She was growing ill. Lie had seeded lie like nascent
pangs into a womb. How distant the heart well knows
is time's forgiveness from the guilt if clothes
the conscience wears can leave us warmth in nothing we believe.
His throat's breath rattle sang the psalm of crows.
On his final bed she wept. Do not look down on grief,
good God, to words I've said or done. Spare the moaning
willow's song if you intend to take your son?

Reminiscing Joe

a

I had imagined him an uncle
stealing home each night
to the Motorola and his own series,
waving down the tanks
on Lenin's square, or barbering
his whiskers to the bathroom floor,
squeaking suds up from the sink.

I had imagined him at prayer
in epaulets and underwear
his buried wife had creased.
When playing games of chess
he'd always snore as if asleep.
Alone, my brother swore, he'd change

the board and play each piece.
I had not imagined him a cheat.
Going off to war, my brother sang,
Each time I love I'm a little old.
There's a bit of Stalin in my soul.

b

I had never seen him pull
his *muzhik* dogs in heat, leash-tight
to teach their memories to heel.
My brother said, he will,
no matter what the fashion
mold their medals out of Gori fields?
When neither showed, Uncle Joe
gave each a collar on his plate
and said we'll never know their minds,
how well they operate.

I had never seen the cossack kicking
the *batushka* round the bathroom floor
with garlands skeined of hanging rope
and hemlock in their cups.
He was our Yalta, our minister of yachts,
all the lords of state we could impersonate.
Coming back from France my brother sobbed,
Each time I hate I grow a little old.
There's a bit of Stalin in my soul.

The Iconoclast

for Alexander Dubček

On a high ridge in the Tatras
far from the Warhol slopes
of Medzilaborce,
I watched a bear
chisel a saint's diluvian face
in the root of a pine
accidentally. This is how
the curator will determine age
and accuracy,
by the artist's teeth marks.
He will happen upon history
in woods such as these, fomented
in saliva and venerated.
He does not know that the hunter,
stalking the lone thicket
for a bent splinter of his precursor,
has already committed the hanging
artist's head
to wood, famously, in order
to mount his map of extinction
on memory
for generations to follow.

Huckster at Noontime

I

In Humenne, in this time of drought,
when the sun and sky
caress like undulating forms,
slow to love in their callow way,

where poets
with fragile appetites and all-day dreaming
twist their spines through jive-talk parlors
like insects through a hammock,

I think of the chrysalis,
how the moth smothers in a spreading flame,
wings itself to death,
too early for the wind.

And I think of the Huckster,
scarred as Tatra rock,
his ring-boned haridelles, blinders cocked,
down at Market Square,
crates of fruit dying early in their season.

2

One day in six,
the red rose wilts in his lapel,
jewels turn to glass on his thumbs,
his wheel rims, rolling free-fall in tall air,
stick fast to the customers, ringing bells
like wards of maternity

for the ripe milk of melons
souring like the odor of hooves and tails.
They have no schedule,
these umbilicates,
exiled in the sleep of their conception.

He spits into nicks of melon bellies,
grinds the sap, the worms,
the spittle of tobacco shreds.
Even corn whiskey turns to gold on his breath.

3

I think of the stench,
the rotten fruit, the cankered skin
like wizened breasts of nuns,
how the juice once flowed,
flesh splitting, wet as lips.

And now this aching
flesh of worms,
blotting the tongue, white,
transparent as onions,
the veins like delicate moth wings.

He plays the martyr, liberator,
the huckster out of season,
dropping apple cores
where now the children lie,
picking roots of rampion
out of the cobblestones of Svernova,
remembering at the cusp of spring,
how bodies back at Wenceslas
rotted red beneath the statue's sword.

II

Yang-Na
(*Los Angeles*)
Many Smokes

And passion rends my vitals as I pass
where boldly shines your shuttered door of glass.

CLAUDE MCKAY

Many Smokes

a

THE BASIN

After naming the ocean "falling breath," they walked
the Appaloosa back, hand to hand, along the basin.
Eyes were shut. No one spoke. The sun, a Chumash eye,

was filling up a cloud above Yang-Na,
and flames of tar pits lent their many smokes
to drifting glades the tribe would name "horizon."

In their polyglot of streams, they found a language,
called it "many tongues," and through its voice
broke the silence down to merging runnels.

Who among them first declined a share of water,
who refused a prophecy or failed to owe his breath
to cranes or condors stroking wings above the wind?

Who would marry nothing less than last predictions
as in quaking earth or the meteor's quotidian run?
Who would lack the vision formed by primal smoke

to steer his horse away from bluffs? Their eyes
had seen coyotes on the slope engrave their faces
in the moon. A hawk entrapped its circling shadow

in the marl and pecked its spine to pillared cliffs.
All earth is sacred ground. A century of whales would scale
the ocean to see the palisades repel the sun.

b

LA BREA TAR PITS

She has learned to hear the mocking throat
clear its stutter underground. She has seen the sleep
fires sweep along the middling and pasadenas,

the smoke muscling through the muted elegance
of clouds high above the cratered stones.
A rib of orange, bold as laughter, follows everywhere

the tribe has gone. Along the wells at La Brea,
she sees the raven bark the rippling water into tar,
a pit as deep in dusk as autumn; in every fall

the death is voiceless: a leaf, a stone,
no matter what the wings, a darkness, a thousand crows
swimming beneath the carp and toads, she believes

that all reflection is a miracle of souls in blossom.
She thinks the water's mirror no more than cloudless sky
and fiercely kicks her horse into the fire's heavens.

She dreams how long a spell the tar will throw,
what dark child will leap into the pit of hunger's birth.
Look now at the daughter waving from the horse

as it leaves the sunlight. Her soul is reflected
in the pitch, in the rills of fire falling from the sun,
a generation of spirits leafing back to earth.

C

FOLSOM

Oh, the streets, the pearled lamps above the courts and hoops
of moons that blaze themselves along the benches. He fears
the arc's perfection, the jump shot's haunted vault

of shoes rising and falling, the ground's hard distance
from the soft sift of the ball through air,
and always the earth in waiting, betraying the leap

with mortal falling, the lost breath of exhilaration
a brother, shipping out to Asian shores, remembers
not as the fast break of a point guard slicing off a pick

nor the ball's slam force gyred through a net,
but the Jordan glide into the infinite *now* of reflection,
a soldier arching stones into a hill of baskets just before death.

Oh, his name, if only to be remembered, faceless
in the chiseled stone, and where the father, lost at birth,
carries cedar sprigs to shape a box, a son is buried

under ground as brittle as the paved courts he mastered
one on one. We are approaching the Avenue of Rocks.
You will recognize it by its tombed passion and its sod.

You will recognize it by the chains hooped and chambered
above the cell's bench slab he climbs to, breathless after dark,
as if all men tossing stars into a basket are equivalent to God.

The Pacific

Its mind has from the little bark of thinking
created the whale, a water tree, a floating
paradox. The ocean seems to believe there is no shore
worthy of thought and beyond the thought no memory.

It has seen the otter's sand diminished, the sea mews tarred,
the mountain space above the beach a swale of fire
burled out of poppies or the greens of weed and kelp
as if persistence by a larger will were reigning,
as if from whales a long thick oak were being carved.

From any distance where the rower steers the waves
away from ground, a reflection enters, breaks apart
and on the stirruped shafts of light, a whale dives up
to branch the shores of memory extinguished in our hearts.

Olvera Street

Chinatown, October 24, 1871

In the evening I met the buckboards
barely rickracking down on warbling axles,
all stacked with laundry under the forked
feet of Chinese coolies, necks tied
to the round of barrels. How many
were there running alongside,
as if they cheered them? The whole city
was in looting for the rancher stilled
by the scrawl of a tong's cross fire.
I took the railroad way, across
the pegs of iron, spikes and hand picks,
and crossed into the ditches
where the sweat-trickles of Asian
skin slicked the sidewalk. Whom should I warn
among the rooters in the street
with their backs to the bailiff's rope,
the coward's sling by which the execution
holds all reason hangman to the law?
Where he stares, unhooded, down to boxes,
the one with wired feet,
too heavy for his rope, leads an oak
behind him broken, with his neck
in train, and dragging both his knees

feeds the police baton his face,
the fifty-first lash, a memory of bones
falling down at birth; he prays
for conviction, to be as hollow as a ghost,
invisible, for the good of the race.

Natural History

Within the pane
barred glass of the city,
there is a child
somewhere in the Museum
of Natural History who is lost,
in awe of nakedness,
who is imagining
a past for the prehistoric skeleton
that no one is allowed to touch
except through memory
to add the flesh on.
When he stands to prayer
at a burial he is where
he goes to take his bones off.

The Walls

The eyes are shuttered. Blinds have dropped
as if to keep the glare and glass from parting.
On Rodeo a thousand bars slide their inch across
the metal stirrups, ride the dull blades

across the backs of bindle stiffs, shapes
and forms leaving for the night, who bundle loaves
of nylons into purses, wallets, none so thick
a payment makes a difference. Nor makes it home.

The backyard panes they pass have cradled
years of crows like eyes of children, staring down
to seeds of ginger grass a Korean gardener
plants as sacrifice to feed his blower.

Out of the back alleys the dayworkers race
like stranded hordes to pry the gates of buses
open. The lone fat cat they butt aside has poked
his found rat into the hedges. It is his right

to fear the transient rising from the Dumpster
who vaults the fence to pick the yarrow,
and like a swallow breeding space, drops to rest
his hollow bones, weaving ivy, thinking it a nest.

A Glass of Claret

She awoke each day to start the engine,
going nowhere but to pause
and see the shadows filling up the garage.
And popping the choke's stiff
indifference, the piping's Rolls exhaust,
she sculpted glass between her lips
and breathing, sipped a flute of pink claret.
She recalled the strains of distance traveled
like a warbling clarinet,
the porcelain sheen of the reed's
loud tunnel, and the basket depth
of her lungs as she shook and creaked.
At noon when the hawthorne strayed
away from skylight, the shade, thumping
down against the oaken door and through,
would crack the mirror above the mantel.
It is then she gathered all the light, to wake
as grateful in astonishment as in shadows
and pretending nothing wrong, would pump
her husband's carbine in the shed.

Hit and Run at the Pantages'

They smash things up and retreat back
into their money . . . leaving others
to clean up their mess.
             F. SCOTT FITZGERALD

I

MANSLAUGHTER

On Hill Street, where once the ash tree
grew like wheat in the valley of ashes,
she heard the rattle of potholes end
the recital of bones beneath the chrome
and hood. From the swift rotation

of wheels now bruised she had only to plead
that bone begets metal begets silence,
and sorrow was enough, if not adored,
that often when she used the Japanese
for gardening, all her mums had died to spores.

Everything in her longed to leap as one
to poll the verdict as if the air had stung.
Did we drive to the Pacific for a new moon

or to be accused of treading on the spines
of those still creeping through our yards

like toads in chorus? But she remained
as silent as the jury in awarding death
its coin. A life is not a life that's taken
in the rain when minds are skidding
and the fog's small eyes slant down.

II

RAPE

And isn't love a *tour de force* to power,
says the lawyer of her husband's lust
for ingenues? Oh, the tearing of her blouse
an actor's ruse, a role he merely played

and won. Miss Pringle surely knew the craft;
the power of art as prayer
that diminishes only by degree of faith.
And isn't theater large enough to show

imagination as inspired? Imagine if,
in the rehearsal of her lines so long repeated,
she had favored as a lostness in us all
the bestiary of our tribal greed. A hunger

for which no wall, no chains, no triple
latch gate could save her from his need.
The fault is hers alone; there are no locked doors
in her upbringing. We walk the center of the road

on double lines because our legs are broken.
She walks both sides, peculiar to the soul
who cannot bear the separateness of the beast
from settling within. The law has spoken.

Shoplifting in a Korean Store

They play hardball in the lot,
stickball in the streets. It was,
after all, the judge agreed, a minor
sport, a little life taken for a slap
across the counter's face,
                    with nothing words
like teasings, distant
trestles lighting up a track,
a sudden switch, a train derailed
barely to be seen. Two invisibles
creating forms the camera lights
                    to fill the screen.
It was as if a silence fell
to shadow a moment in idle talk
between the youth and clerk,
and they were crossed
by an angel, owing in fatigue
to hanging on a word
between the mind
                    and bullet's bark.
No light craned above
the scene, no mirror
to shape the black child's scream
in which the vanishing

debris of all the Asian's fear
could lapse
                backward into memory.
Their eyes had been deceived
by the coarse boot of vision
kicking them out
of an old century. We commend
their common schooling to tape
and bury them
                in commentary
with rarely a thought
the camera saves for sound.
Let the wall shade the dimpled
stale wreath. Let the rain pay
the sod its little coins.
Let the body's small receipt
be a payment to the soil's
fist of fossils
                imaged in the ground.

The Neighbor Who in Found Light

watches, wedged in fog,
the fires lap
the cirrus culms of smoke
on Pico's braided shawl,
his body dumped back
into the punctuation of a question,
surreal and abstract,

who watches the fish hawk
at the swig of a wave
drop a bone
from the bowl of his beak,
curving off into the red
sun of a trawler's squall,

who says we'll take them with us,
like an irritation, the sting
of an eye's ember,
after death, after knowing all
that needs to be known
or done in the nomenclature of doubt,

who sits with his silhouette
on the balcony of darkness,
igniting the body's breath

with fire as the mind's revenge,
unhousing his coiled hardness
with a kiss to the lip of a gun,

who sees the way out
as a chasm, full of light
between his finger and his thumb
where the trigger squats,
taut as a lug,

who bends lower to steer
into his sights, the headlight's beam,
a slanting down of barrels
peculiar to a hunt, no matter
what the chase, or shout,

who finds the flashlight he will light
to be absolved, no longer believing
in stars
as clouding up the firmament,

now shoots into the darkness
of all black hearts
as a right.

The Skinhead

On hearing the Berlin Wall
had fallen, a symbol of nothing
more a wall could do,
he bellies up from his bunker
in the hummock, a lizard Lazarus,
rolling back his rock, tongueless,
more a hiss than a grammar
his wattled throat suspends.
He says that hunger needs a stomach

or a stone the mind can't climb.
So, he finds behind the moats
of pavement a fleet of heads swimming
out, beyond the safe perimeter
of status, stroking, out like flags
from breast to sky, their rigid hands.
How their tongues, cocked back,
applaud the fallen angel's
pitted eyes and hooded skull.

At what moment did he know
we were the weapons, triggered
by our love for flux?
In what shortness of breath
had he known to push

the Ethiopian down a stair
to prove that footing is all,
that, microscopically, any movement
is a centipede with legs,
or that paranoia is a motion, hardly
noticed, idling slow, then fast,
a million years of stutters racing
hatred with fitful starts?

The Docetist

Says that the ragman on the median, washing
clouds with a towel on the glass
he is spritzing, and for no other reason
than to repair the physics of mud and all sins

of remission, is posing, and nothing more,
as an apparition, without body or sense;
this dutiful wraith who suffers only
a pinch of the wind's stone at his back

is accused of knowing that were it a stake,
he would learn, like the Jew who never stepped
foot in Auschwitz but for a passing over,
what is new in the world of revision.

But you be the mouth, you be the rock
and you be the infinite, passing through
like a cold frost cracking stone before the sun
or a tooth in the truth that is daily aching,

and I'll be the dust, I'll be the sound
and like the knotting in the wind's rib,
free the maggot in a fool creating
the ruins of the imagined in the nothing

that's ever found. We are one in this.
Like weary lips that rest, each
on the other, we can taste even in absence
the word at the tongue that is always waiting.

Tajuta
(*Watts*)
The Tower

Rise bloody, maybe not too late
For having first to civilize a space
Wherein to play your violin with grace.
GWENDOLYN BROOKS

The Tower (Nuestro Pueblo)

to Sabato Rodia (1875–1965)

I had it in mind to do something big,
Rodia smiled to think his dome an onion sky,
as he climbed the girders' ground of terra-cotta,
struts of metal wedged between the arm and breast.
What's the use, he thought, to mesh the mortar once
the rain had picked the cobbles clean,
                    what to say
when neighbors called it curious and worse
a nuisance, petty thrift, as steep as trawler masts,
as round as whales? He had failed
nonetheless, for the city's sake to rime
each rung in equidistant scale,
                    and failing order
gave to space the wildness of the thing
as pure in form as latin *trullis*, megalithic
and pristine, as if the light of vision art creates
is nearer to the earth than any law
of rivets, scaffold or machine.
                    What is science
to be owed if ribs of pottery he carves
can build a ladder to the heart? Still he climbed
into the filigree of bottle shells

and giving in to sleep fashioned a horizon
out of stars and follicles of tented clouds, aware
the peacock's tail in the tile's mosaic
                had broken.

Tar

Today you follow the tar
on the wheels of Doheny trucks
with their tin rims glistening
past the tall fires
of hobo cans, the trucks
that poke and race down Croesus Street
as if by name the road
intends a commerce,
as if by hauling
shavings from the coal bins
the debris of ash will hunker
down their long bays
like caught fish thumping
in the throes of ecstasy.

It is your day of delivery,
the "Great Giveback,"
bowls of tar, stacked
free and generously
like barreled water
from the Arrowhead streams.
It is your right, by law,
to receive the pitch
like a sweet syrup
of spun crowberries

to seal the gutter
no matter what your age
or face, no matter how
the lean bank of bricks
has slanted on the sills
against the warped ridge
of a squatting roof.

It is your right to hope
that rain no longer sculpting
the air with its silent knife,
has dried its blade
along the Los Angeles River,
that runnels sipping
on the wheels of the *zanjas*,
are steaming from the weirs
of *brea*, bubbling black.
It is a right to receive
what the land has owed. And not
to have to give back.

It is the tar
renounced by night
that gives you warning
when you look above to see
your mind gnawing bit by bit
into the cracks and trough
of a brilliant sky;

what black moon has splintered down
and in its caulking
seals your small life?
This is the day of deliverance.

A Drive-by on Saeegu

April 29, 1992

She is tall, a child of eight. How will the pistol's
shot create the backfire of a shard of smoke
which throttles through her final thought?
From her shallow eyes the ghosts climb up

to sob above her face; one whose dream, as near
to thinking as the ear, whispers on the lobe
the promise every sun has made, to rise.
The other at her arms, a moon to slow the leafing out
each tree has owed the swinging bough at night.

Both will cross the lids with light
to feed the inner bulbs, believing each will open
out and far. Both, still shining brief enough,
will drive the fused field of breath back into the sky.

And what her years have learned will live in metaphor
through the progeny of sons. Death will give them birth
as when a table in the early sun beads up from feeding
pods of berries to the water in an orchard's eyes.

Dog in the Storm Drain at Florence and Normandie

What was it he clutched, going down,
as he slid between the jaws of the grate,
a sound, perhaps, of teeth grinding,
a slick of rain puddling beneath

as he bled, sucked sudden and swift, a brawling
carcass falling through the rings of hell
into the mere mortal seine of sewage?
What unseemly yelp or wail resists attention

when over ground the Dane and shepherd,
huff and spin, having nipped the bloody
neck for more of the black, Brit Labrador.
They sniff and whimper, each with cycling scents,

the smell of absence, the half-moon
of mutability surviving. The whole city is asleep.
What in the universe had they found him taking,
or breaking all rules, had he trespassed?

The light changes. Red cools to green
and the dogs, bullying the headlights, stake the curb
toward home, obsessed as with history
not with chasing wounds but with territory,

what community the street pretends. His voice
still flows beneath them, once in spillage, twice in echo.
A final stone to the head will not still him.
Laws are little in the world of forgiveness.

Wrought Iron

The lieutenant swears he shimmied up the fence.
A spoke impaled his lungs, and deeper drills

the blood ran out on, coughed the memory up. No one
saw his running pause as if by freezing frames

he could hold the cold expanse of space
between the steepled rods in fists of air;

as if it were his duty now, for camera lens,
to lift his image up to show his past, his face.

He wasn't lost, a black son's dog, or ghetto cat
but only running, climbing as he had to

from the speeding earth, the racing passed
like water down a drain or dizzying down, a momentary

gulp, of thoughts, eluding all of hope, his lips,
his love for believing ground was being gained.

Following the Juvenile Detention Bus

It is raining, the third
wash of glass that fogs
the windshield near his face.
I am caught in traffic turning
Mozart on his back
to reel in tape, and braking,
a distance forming,
the shore of taillights
rushes past, the rain's
teeth, thumb deep
in the flesh of sidewalks,
the swash of blades wiping,
as he should have, his eyes
as he would have the white
panes of glass folding him in
to split the spaces
where only guards could see him
harrowing the streets,
and where he grows
a worry older, certain
that in gaining
five-to-ten, the law was broken.
I am braking, always showing
that in pulling even
to the window grates

that break between us, in this
our collision of eyes,
I am fair
by sharing rain,
the world's upheaval,
spending our noon together
like cedar trees, waving,
touching the window screen
in shadows, darkness,
the ovals of his eyes
splaying through, recalling
the rain's long-tail lightning
like spokes on a spinning needle,
the hard rage of water pricking,
sinking down the sewers
of any alley. And thinking
I am getting out. No matter what
you're thinking.

On the Day of His Death He Dreams

for Ruben Salazar

Today, again he gave up the violin
and turned to walking. A wall
he imagined would inspire him
to stand his back against the earth.
He heard the ground accelerate
its conversation with his feet.
He heard a mason's hand take birth
away from trees. He watched the snow
of a great mind freeze
and the flakes fall like statues.
In his hand the music palled
like any passion which by excess
is confounded. He rammed the bricks
head-on as if in planting
his mind would spawn a seed.
His image in stone survived him.
He lost his sense of hearing
and gained an ear for crossing streets.

With Love the Infinite Is Passing By

after a line by Rilke

At her desk the sobbing came to her
as wires barbing the fists in her eyes,
and with the *banger* in the street
whose brother slapped his coker's cheek
and raced him screaming down the halls
carrying in his palm the swollen lobes
of his bleeding ear, she wept.
In the aching of such wind
came an understanding so unlike
the shouts and tears she knew
while leafing back the light and reading
nights of Baldwin and Bontemps.
In his well of cries she heard her own,
a silent river slubbing down
the floors of Markham High and past
the eastern curbs of Alameda,
where once she ran the crack on wagon paths
that sliced into the troughs
of dust peeling open both her eyes.
And where the ducks had pressed their down
into the mustard weeds, she scoured books
on Selma and the New Ark
down beyond their brittle pricking

to where the burweed staked her feeding.
She had walked herself into their speed
of running, always in pursuit
of words as though they formed a landscape,
scraped and hasped to the tracks
of the Pacific Electric. But in her mind
she will be as the *banger* wants to see it,
nickle-diming and obscene,
conspiring for the weed and smoke,
the mainline, as an accomplice to his kind,
and for redemption to leave all love
for reading books behind.

Meliorism

In her belief that the stonecrop
tends to cling by its water and that she
can dampen its soil, she lives alone
as if in a fist of rocks, the solar
droppings fathering her son;
that by directing the light,
she can expand his vision,
no matter that the pane is dark.
All day she stabs the window,
as if the glare were a country
he could travel without bleeding.
But the stonecrop on the brick
may at least be mapped
by the slow prod of a finger
on a wall. And by a fragrance
near to loam, the senses can remark
how subtle to the nose
grows the itch that worms excite
when sipping in the moist soil.
She senses sight and sound as one.
In all his beauty there is a flaw
she calls perfection. She can hear
the green dark grow along his skin.

Audienca

On Vermont where the flames first burned
her down among the stones, she tells
the captain she cannot
identify the fire in question, that
the riot whistled flight
into its feet. Nor can she remember

any shrub so swift to conflagration
in the valley's poppling heat
as mimosa breathing the wind's still spirit.

In uniform he reminds her of a spoon,
the colonel feeding a hundred
innocents down the throat of a well
in Guazapa. The swallows tarred
the shade stones like griffins,
and no child dared presume
a father bored with sleeping
was alive.

He is not listening. She breathes
each syllable of smoke
into her lungs, afraid

that whispers only
to a dog knee-deep in cactus palm

keep the order of day trivial,
how at dawn siroccos
drain the bougainvillea,
and the patron saint of alms
picks the beggars' pockets.

He has cuffed her hands
down with reminders, this is not
El Salvador. She is illegal.

She wails. And remembers
how she leaped, rape-wise and sure,
with herons into the deep bone well.
The colonel crawled knee and night
to hear her boundaries break.
The swans no longer sleep
beneath the arbor's bower.

She can go to hell, the captain
tells her. She has broken bail.

She shows him what
the fires know of hunger,
there beneath the well's rimrock
where the amaranths grow,
she will show him
Normandie and Jordan Downs.

There where the bethel's light
guides the drover's sheep

above the sedge and spinneys,
she will show him fire, how
at night along the road to Tenancingo,
children parade their cargoes
to the swoon of whippoorwills.
By day the dust of ragged fathers
swell the sea,
contrition for each burial.

She will go to jail.

The Spearwort

The child has found a lost pomander
and within its glass where once the jasmine
roved its hours on a leaf, a ball of amber
where all the fathers go, soon after
birthing and deeper though, much further,
a flower, he imagines, still is thriving
in the sand, being of a stalk
where, in the wind's shadows,
seeds are scattered. Children grow
but never know the spearwort, there
where the sea beats it,
blooms and threshes in the hard
mud. You must imagine all his joy
when off the lowly stem he snaps
the aging leaf and instantly the pod
springs up again. And again,
one after the other.

Purgatorio

a.

TAJUTA

In the first day's dusk
as we drove Ladeira's wide shoulder,
alone, and longing there to know
what looters could not breathe
in the riven sparks of haze,
we saw above the leafing jacarandas
the many smokes of distant coils rising
as if a harvest jeweled its flames
along the banks of the Porciúncula
where once fiestas stocked the mews
of *pobladores* with mounds of melon
and creaking *carretas* hauled Redondo salt.
There the Chumash offered seeds of grass
to tame the marsh *cienegas.*
There along the meadows the sycamores
and alders trickled up from riverbeds,
and grizzlies gnawed on cedar
as if it were a rind of orange
that seeded, needed to be devoured.
So Tereus, needing expiation, devoured
in his frenzy his dearest Itys,
son of his fires.

b.

MUDTOWN

And as those who go
in body but in spirit stay,
we passed down to Charcoal Alley,
where in the mist that cleaved
the red forehead of the sky,
we watched the rain wind in its reel
with no more force than a spigot.
No one knows how first
the Manila Chinos saw the vast
Pacific space, the hypnotic
spin of dark and light
that rained upon the soil
with unblurred uniformity,
if on their spines the derricks
drilled their bits to breed with oil.

On the day that fire swathed the clouds,
we heard the crackling of eucalyptus
ignite the distant barricades
as if some Virgilian urge
had launched all minds into bereavement,
as if, in searching far from the fire's edge,
but for its madness we were so near to it,
raging with Cato on the rock line's scree,
"Are the laws of the pit thus broken
or is there some new counsel
changed in heaven . . .?"

c.

WATTS

Hear now the wisps of flames
scud along the yards like golden terns.
Watch the wind plume them
toward the ocean, rising,
plying the clouds with nocturnal urns.
Listen, as the hot and coarse vapors
begin to seed new planets;
the burrs of the sun will prick
through them. How short a time their hues
endure the raging gases
as if to be mistaken for unruly hell.
We are but faces phrased in voices,
lost vowels in the drift of innuendo
in a city's dream.

But there just where the rock
cracks, see it, there before the huddle
of bones, where the rain has carved
the marl, an olive bark
spires into golden peaks,
and a voice comes craving again
from the cliffs.

Somewhere past the nest of light
a condor wobbles

on his ledge, picking at his wings,
side to side. He breathes
the camphor trails, the swaddling air,
and whining his tail from the flames
swiftly lifts
the furled olive leaf and flutters up,
his feathers thrashing
past the burning barks of cottonwood
and hummocks, blazing
toward the blessed sun.

*The time will come when two golden olive trees
will grow in this city. Their tops will reach
the seventh heaven—and will shine throughout
the world through signs and wonders.*

LIBUSSA

Notes

The Hunger Wall
Charles IV had the poor and hungry build this wall near Prague's Hradčany Castle in order to pay them.

St. Jacob's Church of the Hanging Hand
According to legend a thief, in the act of robbing the Virgin's jewels, was paralyzed until the authorities arrived. The remains of the hand hang in the nave of the church.

Šárka
In Czech legend, Šárka had herself tied to a tree to lure the hunter Ctirad into the forest, whereupon he blew his horn and caused his own death as Vlasta and her militaristic band of women descended on him. Vlasta occupied Devin Castle.

Zivanska
A woodsman's gathering in the forest, characterized by song and food and popularized by Janosik, the legendary Slovak bandit and folk hero.

Many Smokes
Like *Yang-Na*, "Many Smokes" was one of the original names of the Pueblo of Los Angeles.

Hit and Run at the Pantages'
The wife of theater baron Alexander Pantages was convicted and given probation after a scandalous manslaughter trial from 1930 to 1934. During the same period her husband, accused of raping an

actress named Eunice Pringle, hired the celebrated lawyer Max
Steurer for $100,000 and was acquitted.

Tajuta
Like *Mudtown,* "Tajuta" was one of the original names attributed
to the area of Watts in South-Central Los Angeles.

A Drive-by on Saeegu
Sa-ee-gu is Korean for the date April 29 and the term adopted to
commemorate the riots. Forty Koreans had been injured or shot;
an eighteen-year-old college student had been slain amid wild
cross fire.

JAMES RAGAN has lived in Paris, Prague, London, Athens, and Beijing and has been honored here and abroad as an ambassador of poetry. In 1985, he was one of three Americans, along with Robert Bly and Bob Dylan, invited to perform at the First International Poetry Festival in Moscow. He is the recipient of numerous poetry honors, including two Fulbright professorships, the Emerson Poetry Prize, two Pushcart Prize nominations, and the Poetry Society of America Gertrude Claytor Award. He has also been a finalist for the Walt Whitman Center Book Award and the PEN Center West Poetry Prize. He is the author of *In the Talking Hours, Womb-Weary,* and *Lusions,* and co-editor of *Yevgeny Yevtushenko: Collected Poems 1952–1990.* His plays include *Saints* and *Commedia,* first produced by Raymond Burr in the U.S. and later in the Soviet Union. Ragan is the director of the Graduate Professional Writing Program at the University of Southern California.